Naked

Kira J

To order additional copies of this book, contact:
Xlibris Corporation
1-888-795-4274
www.Xlibris.com
Orders@Xlibris.com
122379

DEDICATION

I dedicate this book to Stacey Carter.
You've always been a fan of my writing so now there's an entire
book for you to enjoy

Contents

2007

2008

2009

2011

ACKNOWLEDGEMENTS

What you name you children has a huge effect of how they will grow up. The meaning of the name Shaakira is thankful. I've spent my entire life being just that.

To the most important woman in my life, my mother Suod, I am forever thankful for your constant sacrifices. I once heard "you'll never learn to be woman until you get to see a woman." Because of you I am the woman I am today.

To my father, Frank, no amount of sentences can begin to explain how thankful I am for you. By far the most supportive person I know since I was born. No matter how small or how far fetched my dreams are you always believe they can become a reality.

To my brothers Khalifaa and Malik, no relative or friendship can compare to the bond between siblings. For your contant support and inspiration I am greatful.

To my sister Shanelle, for running to my rescue when things were bad and standing by my side as things were good, I can always take comfort in knowing that no matter who doubts me or how much I fail as long as I make you proud I have already succeeded.

Maisah, you are a part of my family, a part of my friendships, simply a part of me. I am glad to know I can count on you to be a part of this journey too.

Special thanks to everyone who supported me and inspired me in more ways than one.

Christina Worrell, Tori Perry, Deja Thomas, Aquasia White, Celease Martinez, Shaleaha Flowers, Alexander Daniels, Loveya Bell, Ashley Green, Tiffany Page, Sandra and Frank Brandon, Lorraine Wiggins, Tameka Elmore, Dorothy Best, Jessica Sills, Sheira Castillo, and Wilfred Rogers.

UNDATED

Change

How can you be resilient?
When you get let down again?
You gave your heart so many times
But never could get in

It's crazy how you could take them back
And they still push you away
Then when you get tired of being pushed
They want you to stay

You can go back to them again
But they won't act like a lover
They never really fight for you
Until there is another

But things still will not change
They get comfortable and don't care
And when you get annoyed and leave
They wish they had you there

Some things may appear different
At first you'll feel respected
But in time you'll see true colors again
And you'll feel so neglected

It's best to leave on the first offense
Before things get too strange
Or else you'll have to learn the hard way
That they never really change

Fake Smile

There may be a smile on my face
But my hearts hurting like hell
I needed a shoulder to lean on
But there was no one to tell

So I walk out my day as usual
But as best as I can try
Every time I get out of bed
I want to break down and cry

And it feels like this was planned
With the things people do and say
Like they got together in a huddle
And said lets give her a harder day

Or maybe they don't know I'm sad
I do hide it behind lies
They don't know it's not sincere
By the look in my eyes

I had a friend tell me I look sad
And I just sat there sighing
I don't want to bring no one down with me
So I smile instead of crying

At the end of the day when I'm alone
I lay there in denial
Cry inside, die a little
And force on that fake smile

Females

They talk about you to the next man
Then smile all in ya grill
Say they relate to the female problem
When they know they ain't real

Even the ones you don't talk about
Has said something bad about you
And the one you least expect it from
Talks about you too

No matter if you keep to yourself
They talk about you the same
No matter what the subject is
You'll always hear your name

I think 8 out of 10 females
Talk bad behind your back
And when you press them they all say
"I don't got time for all that"

If you think your friends ain't phony
You're obviously in doubt
That's why your names always in something
You know nothing about

So my advice to you is
Don't keep those females close
Cuz' the ones that's with you all the time
Talk about you the most

I Want A Man

I want a man
Who will take the time to realize
Something more than just
Big lips and thick thighs

I want a man
Who's not concerned about all that dough
And wants to invest some education
In his brain for show

I want a man
That could care less about being cool
And reflect all that energy
Towards school

I want a man
That doesn't just sit around getting high
While greater opportunities
Pass him by

I want a man
That looks for answers for every shoulder shrug
And wants to strive to be a man
Over being a thug

I want a man
Who's not afraid to show the public they care
And knows it's important when I cry
For him to wipe that tear

I want a man
I don't have to ask when I want him to stay
And he always knows what I'm thinking
Or about to say

I want a man
Who does what I need to the Tee
But most importantly see he should love me
Just for me

If Nothing Gold Can Stay

If nothing gold can stay
And all pleasure turn to pain
While all life ends with death
And all sun will switch to rain

As yes' become no's
And broken hearts will never mend
Forever's turn to never
And all good things come to end

Summers fall to winter
And the heat subsides with snow
Every love falls deep to hate and so
I have to let him go...

Ms. Understanding

When people make her promises
They don't do all they can
It's ok because it's her
She's expected to understand

Nothing said was ever kept
The ones who made them often found
That she wouldn't make a fuss
It was ok to let her down

She doesn't really like to argue
So she took in the over load
She tried to keep it to herself
She would implode and not explode

Overtime she just stopped asking
Told herself she now was through
They never learned Ms. Understanding
Gets disappointed too

Not To Love At All

The phrase "it's better to have loved and lost"
Is everything but true
Cuz what it takes to get back on your feet
Ain't easy to go through

So to those that are alone
And think they want all the hugging and kissing
I say its better not have loved at all
Because then you don't know what you're missing

One Chance Is Enough

Why the one you love
Always do you foul?
You give them an inch
They'll take a mile

And they leave you at a state
Worst than you are
At the beginning
You still have went too far

Trying you're best
But you can't seem to stop
When you pick yourself up
They just make you drop

Make them your first priority
And they love you last
Keep doing it over
To wash off the past

Your hearts saying one thing
That's not what your head knows
You can always forgive
But you can't let it go

I learned the hard way
And the healing is rough
So for future reference
One chance is enough

One For Mothers

For every breath she takes
I'd sacrifice much more
She wanted access to my heart
But always had her door

To the world she seems to happy
But a smile is her disguise
The smile on her face with the tears in her heart
All come out through her eyes

She goes on with her day
Can't make all happy but she tries
Getting pulled in so many places at once
I know she wants to cry

She feels she's not enough
I can tell she's insecure
I know that she is beautiful
But no one cares to reassure

Someone else would have gave up
But some how she seems to levy
She's taking pills to loose weight
Because the world is getting heavy

I try to make her happy
Because I don't want anything to stress her
She's the solid priceless diamond
That was once coal under pressure

Id give my life for her peace
Even if only for a while
Because I know more than anything
She really needs to smile

Our love is stronger than life
Unconditional, powerful, and real
I hope that it is strong enough
To cause her heart to heal

Save Me From Myself

Everyone is all happy
Hearts of love when yours is stone
Planning ahead for Valentine's Day
And you're all alone

Having had your heart broken
Love ain't something you likely do
Found yourself a brand new crush
But he's taken too

And all your friends you were lonely with
Is out with somebody on track
When your love ain't going no where
What's love when nobody love you back

Found yourself ready to try it again
Considering the good it could bring
But just for sure you learn once more
That love just ain't your thing

Cuz even though there are good times
The pain is to hard to dear
So to avoid the heartache
You'd live out another year

In tears, in hate, in loneliness
All things that's bad for your health
Waiting for the perfect soul
To save you from yourself...

Secret Admirer

His eyes
Like a wild tiger
Waiting to be tamed
I see him all the time

But he does not know my name
His voice
Like a bird singing
Wanting to be heard

I hear him all the time
But we haven't spoke a word
His lips
Like a field of roses

Needing to feel bliss
I feel them in my mind
But we've never shared a kiss
His body

Like a tree
All branched out but in one place
I mesmerize his every inch
But he doesn't see my face

The Mirror

I looked into the mirror
And the mirror looked at me
I felt the constant reflection
And I wondered what I'd see

I told the mirror I was broken
And the mirror did not speak
I told the mirror I was happy
And it knew that I was weak

Some how the mirror always knew me
Even when I told it lies
And even when I looked away
The mirror looked me in my eyes

When I had got my heart broken
The mirror knew just what to do
I had half a heart to live with
And the mirror gave me two

I told the mirror I was cold
And the mirror kept me warm
The mirror was not like common people
It didn't care about my shape or form

The mirror was my constant energy
The mirror was my muse
And when it came to me and others
The mirror never had to choose

The mirror saw my emotions
The mirror saw my soul
And when I thought I'd fall apart
The mirror surely kept me whole

And when my so called "friends"
Tried to push me off my track
I went towards the mirror
And the mirror loved me back

The One That Loved You

I hope you know you hurt me bad
You brought on many tears
I never thought you'd break my heart
After all these years

I thought that we were different
But I lied to myself
There was a time when it was us
There was nothing else

I thought that I could make you stay
But now it seems we're through
I would have gave up every breath
Just to be with you

When I had that smile on my face
You don't know how bad I was feeling
I guess I was covering it then
But this poem here is revealing

When I'm gone you'll realize
Hurting me again was a big mistake
Cuz I'm the only bitch that will ride for you
Those other girls are fake

I can't believe you made me cry
I feel so ashamed
You told me you was gonna "wife" me
But I know now that I got gamed

You won't notice it now
Because those girls think highly of you
But we know them bitches come and go
You let go the one that loved you

The Same

They say the same thing that makes you laugh
Makes you cry
The same thing you live for
Makes you die

The same one you talk to
Will talk about you
The same thing that makes you quit
Help you get through

The same thing that makes you stay
Pushes you away
The same thing that makes you feel good
Ruins your day

The same you fuck wit
Will fuck you over
The same reason you get high
Will get you sober

The same one you learn for
Will just not know
The same one you keep
Will let you go

The same one you turn away
Will always be there
The same one you do everything for
Will not care

So in time you'll realize
That life is a game
It doesn't matter how you play it
Cuz it's all the same

To Love You

To love you
Is to love all of you
From the things you say
To the things you do

To love you unconditionally
No matter what befall
If our happy ending never comes
At least we gave our all

It's to love you when it's oh so right
And still you when you're wrong
To love you extra if you're ever weak
And love you when you're strong

To love you whole entirely
Not just fragments that I choose
To love every aspect of your life
Not caring if you win or loose

All that is important is that you never loose me
Of course I'll always stay
I'd never stray as long as you say
You love me the same way

2006

Suicidal

January 27 2006

If you feel like you keep being let go
And wish someone would hold your hand
If you cry yourself to sleep every night
I truly understand

If you have someone that's says I love you
But the words just don't seem real
If you think things would be better if you were gone
I know just how you feel

If you thought this was a one time thing
But do it everyday
If you want to be around the ones you love
But feel like you're in the way

If you're strong outside but deep down
You want to shatter
If people say the care for you
But you feel like you don't matter

If you want some one to hold you
And you're the type to hold your own
If you feel like doings something crazy
Every time you're left alone

If you wondered who would be there
If you had issues with your health
If you want to brake down and cry out to someone
But keep it to yourself

If you think one day it's gonna end
But know that's not true
If you think no one knows how you feel
I'm going through that too...

Too Good To Be True

April 19 2006

Somewhere over this time
While trying to be free
I missed my chance and wounded up
Right where I didn't wanna be

I'm waiting to wake up
From this dream that I'm in
To come across the nightmare
Where you hurt me again

It's not like I don't want to be happy
I just thought I knew you well
But it seems you have surprised me
In love you can never tell

I hear you say you love me
And I know I love you too
But as perfect as we are
I know it's too good to be true

Appreciate

June 27 2006

You can never appreciate company
'Til you're lonely
Never appreciate real people
'Til there's phonies

Never appreciate money
'Til you broke
Never appreciate easy breathing
'Til you choke

Never appreciate sight
'Til you blind
Never appreciate sense
'Til you lost ya mind

Never appreciate freedom
'Til you bared
Never appreciate food
'Til you starved

Fell In Love With You Again

September 26 2006

I'm seeing you for the first time
We're sharing our first kiss
Every time you leave me
My heart is filled with miss

Playing silly games
Stomach getting butterflies
Falling asleep together
As I'm looking in your eyes

Joking with each other
Talking all night long
Asking stupid questions
Feelings growing extra strong

Trying not to do this
But the truth defeats pretend
I washed away our past
And fell in love with you again.

Nobody Cares

October 2 2006

I sit alone in my room
Crying my silent tears
Not a knock at my door
Cuz nobody cares

My feet are so heavy
I couldn't walk up the stairs
I fell back, no one to catch me
Cuz nobody cares

It would be different if it were days
But it's been a few years
No one to rescue me from time
Cuz nobody cares

Going around the same shit over
Playing musical chairs
No one to stop me in my cycle
Cuz nobody cares

Every time I look for comfort
I get judgment and stares
No one to let me cry on their shoulder
Cuz nobody cares

I sit back and listen
To people tell me their fears
I never get my chance to talk
Cuz nobody cares

I took the time to write this poem
To see if anyone hears
And after reading all of this still
Nobody cares

2007

Cry For Help

January 3 2007

He not necessarily asked for advice
But I took it upon myself
I thought the brick wall attitude
Was a desperate cry for help

I put time effort and energy
Toward leading his life right
But if I keep trying to dry an ocean
I'll severely lose that fight

I pondered every tactic
Yelling, begging, cries, all the above
He took every material thing I could offer
But wouldn't intake my love

For every hug and kiss I threw
He just threw out a punch
His resistance head on with my persistence
Made my words nothing but letters in a bunch

I tried to open his eyes
To all the good that could come to his life
He was just so discouraged by darkness
That he couldn't believe in sight

Always being led to believe
That the best things were far out of range
He could buckle down and rejoice the pain
But was far unaccustomed to change

Everyone tried to persuade me
To let him drown in his piss
But the love I had was far too strong
For me to resort to this

My happiness thrived off his
So I put his well being before mine
I looked sadly upon that brick wall one day
There was no love for me to find
I tired to continue this one sided love
Maybe something in this could fulfill me
As he grew sad I grew much sadder
Loving him so much it could kill me

I realized one day it was dangerous
For us to be apart
Cuz if something were ever to happen to him
It would surely stop my heart

So I continued watering up my plant
With the waters from my eye
No flower could ever sprout from this dirt
Cuz the roots were far too dry

If I got him out of a tight situation
He'd go get in ten more
If I saved him from a deadly virus
He'd throw away the cure

Maybe he would hurt himself
As a way to get to me
All my attempts and frequent failures
Was his way of breaking free

Realizing there's nothing I could do
If he kept on refusing my boat
We parted ways I looked back on his face
As im hoping that he'd stay afloat

I couldn't have told him enough
That there's good out there to be found
I couldn't be his life saver
When he was always bound to drown

Unbroken

January 8 2007

His kiss is like a thunder storm
That washes my hurt away
To make eye contact with him
Is to know everything will be ok

For him to hold me in his arms
Will be all the shelter I need
Love way beyond comparison
We started a new breed

His coat of love is my umbrella
Than can with stand any rain
His voice is stronger than any aspirin
Taking away my every pain

His touch gives me amnesia
Causing me to forget my past
My heart went from not beating at all
To beating extra fast

The things he says will move me
Send my body in a trance
Snatched away my "fuck love" attitude
And gave my heart a chance

He fought the battle to my heart
Though I was reluctant to let him try
Put laughter smiles and sincere love
Where there used to be a cry

He loves me at every angle
Physical features and within
Got me far from stuck on hate
Took my emotions on a spin

My first thought was this is too good to be true
Because no one really cares
But he holds the knife that cuts the tension
And sliced away all of my fears
Couldn't have asked for better
Tears had caused my eyes to tire
His love is visine to my eyes
That let me see my hearts desire

If I had ten cents for every time I felt this
I'd have a dime
I know it's dangerous to hope
But I hope it's for real this time

He once brushed past me as I walked
And it left me at and angle
Knocked straight off my feet realizing
I'm in the presence of and angel

He wanted to start a love train
So he went and got the token
Only the love we share together
Could make my heart unbroken

Secret Escape

February 12 2007

Her secrets stay hidden
In the depths of her soul
A lot of emotions built up in her
But she lacks the one that makes her whole

Eyes cover heavy burdens
That sealed lips will never crack
Tries to drown the loudness of the past
But the silence keeps them coming back

Colors even reflect a memory
So her eye lids rarely part
No way to escape when you can't face
The lightness or the dark

She concealed her secrets in a jar
And put them on a shelf
With no where to turn hide and run
When you're trapped inside yourself

They say the structure of a skirt
Is discovered in its seams
She can't escape secrets in her sleep
They convert into her dreams

Hoping that a fire will come to burn t
His secrets in the jar away
Is the way she resorts to knowing the fact
That there will come a day
That the shelf will break and the jar will shatter
And the secrets that once were untold
Will spread out of the fragments of glass on the floor
All they will begin to unfold

Her secrets are silent in the ears of others
But in hers they seem to shout
Like a kettle cooked up but the steam in her soul
Has no way of escaping out

So until the shelf breaks from up holding her weight
She will use all her features to hide
Exhales air, cries out tears, and let's go of her fears
But her secrets still remain inside

Saliva

February 12 2007

You are saliva
I can try to spit you out
But naturally more of you generates

My mouth feels it can do without you
As it's begging to be left dry
Though I might die this way

I'd rather that than swallow
You or let you fill my throat
With all of you
Saliva-till I choke

Weather

April 25 2007

I am the weather
I never stay the same
At any given moment
I can go from sun to rain

When I get upset
And feel like taking something under
Hail, lightening, and blistering cold
Follows right behind the thunder

I often find myself
Not knowing where to flow
Dropping pieces of myself everywhere
Simply flowing like the snow

I'm hardheaded and unpredictable
Sometimes I never learn
To keep a cloud with me
Instead of causing things to burn

When I get really emotional
Major factors drift away
The sky is not black blue or purple
Everything seems so gray

When I get dull and lonely
My hearts in need of a mend
Everyone's out skirts flying up
While im flustered like the wind

Some days I get confused
About how things should form
Starting hot moves to cool
But somehow always ending warm

But when I finally do feel happy
It illuminates everyone
Not to need coats and umbrellas
And to finally see the sun

I Wish

May 22 07

I wish I didn't have eyes
So I couldn't see
I wish my emotions would die
So I could be free

I wish my eyes would dry up
So my tears wouldn't fall
I wish my body went numb
I'd feel nothing at all

I wish my days were fulfilling
So my heart won't be hollow
I wish I could erase yesterday, now,
And tomorrow

I wish time would stand still
So my pain wouldn't grow
I wish I was unaware
Free from all that I know

I wish I caught amnesia
Forgetting all of my past
I wish I was resilient
And got over this fast

I wish my feelings coincided
With the words that I say
More than anything in this world
I wish I'd go away

I wish the hours would race
So each day won't drag on
I wish I stopped myself
Before I became so far gone

I wish I could go back
And change every mistake
I wish I had no heart
So it couldn't break

I Used To Believe In Love

May 22 2007

I used to believe in love
A smile was in my range
Now since I have grown accustomed to this
I've learned that it won't change

I used to believe in love
That's all I could pray for
But this is no boast the ones I loved most
Have all walked out the door

I used to believe in love
Even when it was hard to feel
Now it's been gone for so long its so out of reach
That it just seems unreal

I used to believe in love
Even when it made me cry
I put my all into it but love
Would never even try

I used to believe in love
Somewhere it's gone astray
We set out on this life trip
But love died along the way

I used to believe in love
Now I can't tell the real from fake
Everyone wants the real thing
But it all cost your heart to ache

I used to believe in love
Til' it turned my heart to stone
Now it hard to tell what's worst
Being in love or being alone

I used to believe in love
Now it's been to dark to see
Why waste my time believing
When love never believed in me...

Fall in Love Alone

May 23 2007

My head can't say I hate you
'Cuz my heart knows that's a lie
I can't stop myself from caring
Even though I always try

Just seeing you with other girls
Makes my body shake
Freezing the few fragments left of my heart
And causing them to break

Not only do they shatter
But the things you do and say
Has the ability to collect what's left of me
And sweep what's there away

You don't want me, leave you alone
Those two things I have to grasp
My hearts put under pressure
'Cuz I fell for you too fast

It's killing me to know that
It will never be like before
I try to distance myself from you but
It just makes me love you more

I've accepted that I love you
In my own distorted way
You got that certain thing about you
That can always make my day

I can't say I'll die without you
I will manage to get by
But the thought of losing you itself
Makes me break down and cry

In thought I could never really loose you
Why do my emotions pay the cost
If I never really had you
Then there's nothing to be lost
I really miss the way we used to be
Things have changed from now and then
I just knew that I would fall for you
It was hard to stay your friend

This out come is my fault and problem
Effecting only my mood and tone
Once I again I do this to myself
And fall in love alone

Letters To An Old Friend

June 12 2007

Every time I try to get over you
I flashback to all of the things I'm gonna miss
And it sucks to have to go through this process again
The whole "get over him' thing because
It's been so hard getting over him
And you helped me get over it
So now I have to get over you?...

When people ask me about you
I just tell a lie
Because the question in the back of my mind
I just wanna know why?
Would you go from being the person that I wake up to
To the one who makes me cry

And it's not like I did anything to you
I was the only one who could see right through you
But it amazes me how we barely speak
And you act like I never knew you

I'm the one who you would talk to for hours on the phone
Up till we both got extra tired and had to go to sleep
Cuz we knew we had to meet up the next morning
Yea that was me

Now it seems you hate me
It's not like we lost touch
I never knew someone could hate me so much

Even when I'm just saying hi
You hurt me and don't even try
Something so simple as looking me in the face
Sucking you teeth and passing me by

All my friends say forget you
Believe me I've been there
I can't tell you about it
Cuz I know that you don't care

It's killing me to have to throw away all of our past
Cuz what we had was rare
I was able to move on
Against all of my fears

I tell you I miss you a million times
But my words fall on deaf ears
If you choose not to return I'll wait as many years
It takes to cry a river
I'll be drowning in my tears

I'm Not In Love With You No More

June 18 2007

I'm not in love with you no more
I know you don't believe me
I guess my feelings finally caught up
From all the times that you would leave me

I'm not in love with you no more
I'm done with all the pain
I'll always have some love for you
But I don't love you the same

I'm not in love with you no more
I'm tired of being torn
I bet you haven't noticed yet
This time I'm really gone

I'm not in love with you no more
I gave us my best try
But I'd rather be with someone
Who makes me laugh not make me cry

I'm not in love with you no more
I can't keep being a regretter
I guess I finally woke up and noticed
That I can do so much better

Inaccessible

June 19 2007

When I want you to come see me
You're always busy
Like your phone line
When I really need to talk
You're always tired
Like the excuses you make
When I really wanted to see you
'Cuz I had a bad day
Not to bitch or tell you anything extra important
Just to feel ya presence
Be around you if only for a minute
Because you got somewhere to go
I just need to see those arms and be held in it
Affection is good to show
And when I call you after 12
And you don't pick up it hurts
'Cuz that's when I need to hear your voice the most
And no, not the voice on your answering machine
When you keep forwarding my calls to voicemail
Can't you tell I'm tired of sleeping on your promises
I'm ready to wake up to better things
Not different in physical sense
Just in your certain reaction to me
I just wish we could be

Letters From a Crazy Girl

June 19 2007

I didn't think I'd end up here
I've been keeping my thoughts clean
I'm tryin' to keep my cool this time
But I'm feeling like a fiend

I've got a few ways to reach you
Through ya friends, or I could call
If I cant contact you through one
It makes me try them all

I've grown well out of my stalker ways
My binoculars are on lock
Though there are those impatient days
I stumble through your block

But that only happens on a day
I really need to see your face
If could get to my computer
Id be checking you're my space

Don't get me wrong I'm not obsessed
I just love to look at you
I go to ya page to my favorite pic
And stare for an hour or two

Had anyone else been blowing me off
Someone would have been taken their spot
But I can't contemplate replacing you
'Cuz you're so freakin' hot
And not the hot that you see everyday
When you stand next to me its mutual
'Cuz you're just as hot as me
And they don't make us like they used to

I'm thinking of going to Madame Tussans
To get a life size you
The fact that you'll be made of wax
Restricts the things I'd do

I hope I don't sound crazy
You have no need to be afraid
I'm just a girl who makes herself a toy
That begs you to be played

When I Left You

June 27 2007

Tantrums became laughter
Eyes went from wet to dry
All my frowns turned into smiles
No longer do I cry

In the public eye at least
I don't let my feelings show
It seems as though I'm over this when really
I was crying a few minutes ago

I deal with the internal conflict
The battle of staying or leaving
I learned the difference in dying emotionally
And physically stopping my breathing

But when I left you I expected
That would repair my emotional health
While trying to find the love in you
I lost my entire self

It's safe to say it was for the best and worst
It's only determined by each days break
The best possible thing that could happen to me
Was yet still my worst mistake

Fair Exchange

July 18 2007

These pieces of my heart right now
Are all that I posses
But the love in them allows me
To give you all the rest

If I could love you whole
That what I surely do
And if had a heart to give
I'd give it all to you

Its true that it was broke before
Each day my heart decreases
As time looks for me to find someone
Who will find the missing pieces

Every time I loose a piece
I push someone away
Just to keep what's left of me
When I really want them to stay

The pain I felt before
Makes it hard to let you in
But I realize by giving up
I'd be letting that pain win

So for you and only you
I'll risk my heart losing its tact
I'll give you these few pieces
If you give me yours back

Sixteen

August 28 2007

The things I've been through recently
Still linger in my head
I caught myself trying to save a love
That was already dead

As I was longing to be happy
I saw myself trying to freeze a smile
Saying things as if I'm sure
But with everything I'm in denial

I trusted someone with my heart
That I barely even know
All the issues I've been clinging to
I finally let them go

I've accepted what's in front of me
And what's not yet in range
I've decided to run away from
All the things I cannot change

Two Hearts

August 28 2007

Our situation scares me because
The last person I gave my heart
Did everything in his power
To break it all apart

It took me a very long time
To piece it together with staples and glue
And just as I was finishing
I got stuck on to you

This distraction made it difficult
To finish my hearts chores
That's why I'm glad we're glued together
'cause now I've got a piece for yours

But what scares me is not knowing
That if our bondage comes undone
You're taking your whole heart with you
And I'm back to having none

Glue and staples never held up anything
That ever really stayed
So we need concrete for my heart to beat
I'd no longer be afraid

So I'm hoping while we're stuck tight
You're willing to put in time
I keep you're entire heart in tact
As you work on building mine

Love At First Sight

November 9 2007

I tilted my head up
And gave the room a glare
The world around me disappeared
And only you were there

Your presence and mine clashed
As the room was filled with depth
So over whelmed with ecstasy
I quickly lost my breath

So I waited for the click
For our souls to intertwine
I counted down from 10 to 1
Then your eyes met with mine

This was one of those moments
When everything's so right
You and I both knew
This was love at first sight

Not Wanting

December 10 2007

This not wanting to cry
Subsides my honest ways
Keeps me flurried mixed emotional
And sends me on a daze

This not wanting to fight
Locks in all that is I
Imploding not exploding
Which just makes me want to cry

This not wanting to wait
Keeps me anxious deep in sorrow
This staying awake today
Makes me sleep throughout tomorrow

This not wanting to starve
Is often confused with greed
I don't have hunger for my wants
It's solely what I need

This not wanting to hurt
Keeps my true feelings at bay
'Cuz for all the pain to go away
I know I couldn't stay

This not wanting to accept
Sends my mind on many trails
Back and forth with yes and no
Just keeps me in denial

This not wanting to wake
Is the most of my desired
'Cuz if I could sleep forever
I'd no longer be so tired

2008

Bitterness

January 31 2008

Disappointed bitterness
Stays up all night alone
She had a long day with defeat
So now she waits for pain to come home

As she roams throughout her day
She reminisces to let time fly
Misery's her only company
She and love never saw eye to eye

As the sky goes black to white to gray
Bitterness pays all her dues
Filling broken hearts with blues
They never get a chance to choose

Because what does she have to loose
By snatching un-tattered souls with glee
Turning love to hate and hate to hurt
With not one ounce of sympathy

Or apathy or anything
That would cause the norm to jitter
Her "fuck you" view don't care who's who
Might be what keeps her bitter

In a sense she just gave up on love
On happiness on bliss
But one thing she can't dismiss is this
Her state of bitterness

Naked

March 28 2008

I feel naked when I'm with you
Not the naked I know most think I'm referring to
But the kind of naked that has my emotions bare
Not my body
I feel like I can cry around you
And not feel
Like you feel
Like I'm just having one of those female moments

You make me feel naked
No longer trapped behind clothes
Closed eyes
Closed doors
Or closed lips
Because I feel like I can tell you everything
From tales of my first kiss
To my deepest secrets

Baby you make me expose myself
Wanting to show you every single stitch and inch of my soul
Show you the whole me
Express to you when I am lonely and need you
Baby you make it ok to admit that I need you

'Cuz I'm so used to
Putting up a front
Mixing up those things in life I need
With my momentary wants
But you've dug down to my most raw materials
Honestly—you've gotten to the science of me
To where I'm no longer mixtures and compounds
You've found the elements of my heart
Let's go back to the start

I feel naked when I'm with you
The kind of naked that makes me wants to skinny dip
Into rivers of love
Of you
Of us
'Cuz I trust this
And that's uncommon for me to do
Because I've never had someone love me
Then again I've never been with you

Or had a clue
About what was true
Until you came along to love me
The way you wipe away the tears and hurt
When life attempts to scuff me

It's just so powerful
You do things nobody else knows
How to do
Or what to do
That mentally blows off all my clothes

Now this is what you call naked
I'm bare-exposed-revealed
And you still love me
So it must be real
I'm unsealed-with no shield- and I feel
Naked

To Touch and Be Touched

April 18 2008

To touch and be touched
Is to kiss and be kissed
To love and be loved
To miss and be missed

To feel and be felt
To hold and be held
To snatch and get snatched
You reach I reach back

It's a mutual love
That always reveals
That feeling you have
That gives you the chills

It's to hug and be hugged
To fight and get fought
To grant and make wishes
To fall and get caught

To need and be needed
To be and let be
To cry for and cry with
To be saw and to see

To talk and to listen
To stay or to leave
To push and to pull
To give and receive

An exchanging of smiles
Or a glance for a glance
For having a moment
Or taking a chance

To the tear that you drop
Because you love them so much
Oh how it feels
To touch and be touched

I Fell

June 17 2008

I fell....

So fast
So deep
So hard
Cant sleep

So rare
So real
So bare
To feel

So nice
So true
So me
So you

So high
So far
Just where
We are

So smooth
So rough
Can't get enough

So calm
No fuss
So sweet
So us

So light
So hot
It hits
The spot

So plain
So swell
So fast
I fell...

The One I Can't Obtain

October 3 2008

It always seems that when it comes to me
Desire always taunts
Giving me my life's entire need
But never any wants

From the very 1st day I saw him
I wondered if he was up for grabs
How ironic it seems the only one I want
Is the one I can not have

It kills me not to take him
And embrace him with a kiss
To hold him close and let him know that I
Could fill his life with bliss

But this dilemma stretches beyond me
And my life's most daily challenge
It would never be just him and me
When three hearts hang in this balance

I've never been so patient
And it grows thin as I restrain
Trying not to fall in love
With the one I can't obtain

Coping
October 7 2008

Every time I'm forced to shed a tear
It seems I am reminded
That there are things that I don't need to see
Love really leaves you blinded

And every time I loose someone
Externally I stay strong
While I internally melt away
You never realize what you have till it's gone

And it hurts just that much more
I'm not the strongest but I try
To shield my heart from everyone
So no ones ever seen me cry

Most times I'm stuck inside my head
Just to avoid what I feel
Getting lost in my imagination
Is how I escape what's real

But the real is just that more pertinent
For it brings my life such sorrow
We all must cherish every moment
Since no ones guaranteed tomorrow

And if only for a moment
Should we reminisce on the past
While maintaining our present
Because the future came too fast

Me, Myself, and I

October 21 2008

Staying to myself
'Cuz I'm the only one I know
I always know how I feel
Even when it doesn't show

I know I'll never hurt me
I know I'll never lie
I know that I can trust myself
To never make me cry

Yet still I know that I am beautiful
I know I am divine
I know that I will never leave
'Cuz I am only mine

I feel this is permanent
I feel this is for sure
I feel so happy with myself
I couldn't be more secure.

Tree

December 9 2008

They say green is the color of envy
But green is all she knows
Over time she will discover brown
And maybe others while she grows

She blows with wind but stays planted
For her roots are in the ground
And no matter what she misses
She will never turn around

She soon found one day while looks down
Those good things lived there under
But no amount of sun could keep her safe
She conducts lightening that follows thunder

She always has to fear the fire
And those that chop her for there cause
They throw her in their flame for warmth
Or use her on their floors

Everybody tends to flowers
No one sees what she can be
They don't notice her potential
'Cuz who could ever love a tree

2009

W

October 5 2009

So love him more than words can say
More than actions could ever show
More than trees could ever grow
And more than he could ever know

Loving him is such a pro
And I have yet to find a con
'Cuz when his eyes entwine with mine
I know I'll love him for all time

It's hard to fathom such a love
'Cuz before us there was no such
No level to ever touch
This length of loving him so much

In his clutch he holds a beating heart
I never thought was real
After being numb for quite sometime
I finally can feel

2011

Beauty

February 6 2011

I just took a walk alone in the rain
Early morning, not a sound
I took in the air and look down to stare
At the rainbows on the ground

All greatness it seems that only in dreams
You find beauty to fit every eye
It goes beyond faces to unusual places
Not all angels reside in the sky

Average

February 21 2011

We never aim for the high standards
We're all content with the "at least"
Always getting the small portions
Never once a chance to feast

Everyone's cool with mediocre
No one wants to live life lavish
It's ok to not stand out in a world
Where everyone is average

To afraid to be on the bottom
That we don't reach for the top
I participate in silence thinking
When will the cycle stop

All the knocked up girls and the locked up boys
I see it again and again
Who can you possibly send to defend
Against something they can't win

Bunch of medium thinking people
No one dreams big or little
They don't live above or below
Just staying in the middle

Just the same as those around you
Yet most often end up boasting
You can never truly be your best
When everyone is coasting

I wish there were more takers
That don't get weighed down by baggage
Staying afloat and off the boat
Where everyone is average

Life Is Like A Roach

February 24 2011

Of all of my observations
I've learned life is like a roach
Its ok, it could be better
Kinda like when flying coach

There are lots in common with the bug
Though our lives are not quite equal
Most have that roach effect
Pop up when no one wants to see you

Running around all day
Rarely getting a job done
Often cut short in our advances
When people fuck with you for fun

Knowing something's is inevitable
You can't escape you doom
The young black life and the roach
Both lives ended too soon

Writers Block

February 27 2011

Its hard being poet
When its you against the clock
Rambling on writing nonsense
As you're faced with writers block

I put the pen to paper
In my efforts to coerce
But poetry like love
Is something that can't be forced

I bounce back and forth through topics
But I just wasn't inspired
I've ate so its hunger
And I've slept so I'm not tired

I tried to make the best of this
But all good things come to end
So to save you guys from a crappy poem
I'm putting down my pen

Water Works

March 13 2011

If I evaporated would I leave a trace?
Would you remember this face?
Or would the world keep spinning
As if I never had existed
Would you miss this?
This moment
This memory of me and us
Would the ground still be wet?
To show that even though I am no longer here I rained
Would it all be the same?
The thing of water is it comes in many forms
Have many charms
So would I still be thought of if you couldn't hold me in those arms?
See it's sad to say one day the sun will come
To shift my state
And I'm not gonna be a puddle
I'll have to follow my own fate
I'll always mist over you when I'm up in those clouds
So let's just cherish the rain while we have it for now

The Years

September 11 2011

I been in love with the same man
Since I met him
That was back in '07
Just ain't know how to tell him

Gave him the time of day
Everything was so great
He stole all my attention
Back in '08

Even though we were serious
Everything was still fine
I made that man mine
That was back in '09

More than a lover
He became a best friend
One of our best years
That was 2010

So here we are now
Between hell and heaven
Still making it last
In 2011

To the years that's behind us
And the years that will come
I still love him the same
As if this was year one

Love

October 23 2011

No one knows what it sounds like
Its something you can't hear
Its volume varies with each person
And it changes with every ear

We can't speak on what it looks like
No matter what comes across your screen
It's something we all know exist
But it can not be seen

No one can be exempt from its effects
By choosing when you fall
Or who or why or when you fall
It just affects us all

No one can put it into words
Though it may linger in your head
It's more something that is done
Than something that is said

Half Empty

December 6 2011

Lately I been feeling half empty
Like a bottle on a shelf
Half of me is here
The other half is somewhere else

I'm 50 percent happy
The goodness last throughout the night
But when the sun comes it brings to light
That during the day I'm not alright

I love my partner 100 percent
But here is where we disagree
I gave him my entire heart
Now there's no love left for me

It's unhealthy to love someone more than yourself
That's the setup for heartache
Eventually your soul will break
It's only so much pain one heart could take

Sadly leaving hurts more than staying
It just makes the mind go grim
So you survive off the love your project
Reflecting off of him

Because he never really loved you
It's proved with every indiscretion
He just knows he can control you
'Cuz your hearts in his possession

He has more of an obsession
Still stuck in his childish days
With such evil tricks he plays
He gets them with his charming ways
So how can you truly fault the many girls
For what he put you through
He told ya'll the same lies and so
She might just love him too

And that's the thing about this boy
He will knock you right off track
You could love him more than life itself
He still won't love you back

You find yourself feeling half ugly
Half stupid in the brain
100 percent insecure
100 percent insane

College

December 7 2011

College is not for everyone
It sure is not for me
At this age my focus is completing my goals
So I can live worry free

There's so much I want to do in life
So many barriers I wish to pass
People never understand me when I say
Its some things you can't learn in a class

Yes I know I'm VERY smart
I learn at a fast pace
But just because I'm not in school
That doesn't mean my mind will waste

I would never enter into something half way
Just so I could be accepted
And I tend to follow what's best for me
And not just what's expected

My motivation is my happiness
I give myself the fuel
It's so much more to being accomplished
Than just going to school

And how could I be successful
If I give up being me
Put aside my drive for what I love
To get an unwanted degree

A lot of people tell me im weird
Because I never follow the norm
In a world where everyone is pupated
I just will not conform
Most students are just there to be there
I stopped and did an evaluation
It makes no since to put in time
If you have no plan after graduation

A lot of my friends and family are in school
So don't think I'm a college hater
I just can't see myself giving four years
To get a piece of paper

Some may be mad by that last statement
I don't wish to confuse them
But degrees only means something
To those that plan to use them

I know it's smart to always have plan b
But you must consider the facts too
There is no age limit on going to school
That is something you can always go back to

I'm blessed to have great talent
That I combine with lots of knowledge
The moral of the story is
Stop asking why I'm not in college

Things You Accept

December 11 2011

I'm sick of myself
And all the things that I endure
For always letting hurtful people
Walk in and out the door

I'm sick of hurting myself
When he fails to cover his track
And I'm sick of complaining about a boy
That I keep on taking back

I'm mad I me for not
Being strong enough to let go
I'm upset that he's still cheating
And I'm pretending I don't know

I'm mad because I want to leave
But I never work up the nerve
And I'm disgusted that I settled for this
When I know what I deserve

I'm upset with my heart
For taking over and controlling my brain
I'm sick of finding dirt
Just for it to be in vain

I'm sick of crying all the time
Lately my pillow has gotten wetter
I'm pissed I let myself be stupid
When I know I was taught better
I'm sick of arguing and fighting
About promises that aren't kept
I'm mad that I blame him
For all the things that I accept

I'm sick that I just noticed this
There's no better time than now
To take responsibility
For all the things that I allow

I'm sick that I still love him
This revelation is strange
Because even though I just confessed
I know nothing is going to change

I Write

December 20 2011

Some guy asked me what's the purpose of my poetry
And I simply said expression
To invite you into my most inner thoughts
Each poem is a confession

And after he asked me that he said
What makes your words more real
I strive to write something you can feel
But also it can heal

I write to make that day easier
When you feel everything is over
I want you to read my words
And it be the reason you stay sober

I write to ease the pain
From all the pressures that collide
I write for everyone who ever
Thought about committing suicide

I write for all the people who think
They cant stand on their own
I write for all the girls
That's in relationships alone

I write for everyone
Who keeps their feeling on a shelf
I write for people with no support system
And you only have yourself

I write to be and outlet
When the world just takes a toll
And when you're up 'cuz you can't sleep at night
I write to calm the soul

I wrote to provide realness
When everything around you is fake
I write to be the remedy
When things cause your heart to ache
I write to block the bad
And get you focused on the good
I write to relate to you
When you feel misunderstood

I write to get it out
And confess to all my fears
I write to provide smiles
In the place of all the tears

And even though I write to block the tears
We need them to get by
I write to tell the strongest hearts
That it's ok to cry

I write to insert strength
To every place that you feel weak
I write so you can read the words
That you're afraid to speak

I write 'cuz in this day and age
Thoughts can't stay in my head
So I write so I have no regret
For what I could have said

I write for everyone
Who's been taken advantage of
I write for all us heartless girls
That's given up on love

I write because I see
That when you're smiling its for show
I write because I get
That it's not easy letting go

I write to fill the silence
When there's words that cant' be spoken
I write to put you back together
If ever you feel broken

I write to give you air
When you just can't catch your breath
I write to make things right
When everything just takes a left
I write to lift your spirits
When the world just keeps you down
I write to give you company
When no one is around

I write because I've been through things
And my story must be told
I write to release the pressure
Of the standards we uphold

I write because this is my life
And it's no where near through
I write because though we are different
I'm just the same as you

CPSIA information can be obtained
at www.ICGtesting.com
Printed in the USA
FSHW011924021020

9 781479 716609